About Daniella Blechner

Daniella Blechner is the author of *Mr Wrong* and the poetry anthology *7 Shades of Love*. She's passionate about inspiring and empowering women through the sharing of stories, identifying and challenging negative belief systems and patterns, and unleashing the True inner voice.

After experiencing a decade of dating disasters, Daniella decided to look within and challenge her own belief systems about love, relationships and most importantly, herself. She is a firm believer that if you keep attracting the same types of people, circumstances and situations into your life, a serious inner journey needs to be made to identify, examine and challenge negative belief systems.

Mr Wrong is an insightful and witty exploration into why some women repeatedly encounter Mr Wrong and toxic relationships. It is a collection of real life relationships stories written by women who have encountered the infamous Mr Wrong as well as success stories and stories from men, too. Do men get a bad rap? What role do women play? Through questionnaires, quizzes and reflections, Mr Wrong allows space for readers to reflect upon their own dating experience and identify patterns for themselves.

As Einstein so prophetically stated, *"Insanity is doing the same thing over and over again and expecting a different outcome."*

7 Shades of Love is a collection of poems written by an eclectic mix of women and men around the globe on the Universal theme of Love. On a quest to explore exactly what Love is, Daniella draws connections between the seven colours of the rainbow and the vital chakras, exploring Eastern and Western associated meanings of colour and connecting them to Love.

Daniella Blechner is also a teacher and healer who puts her Heart into everything she does. She is currently running one day workshop *7 Steps to Creating the Greatest Version of YOU* a one day workshop for women who want to create and be empowered and *Unleash Your Voice*, a six week workshop that helps women to unleash their own voices and begin a journey towards publishing their own memoirs.

Daniella also does one-to-one book coaching via face-to-face meets or Skype.

www.daniellablechner.com
www.dingdongitsmrwrong.com
info@daniellablechner.com

7 Steps to Creating the Greatest Version of You: Daniella Blechner.

Non Fiction Self Development Work Book

Copyright © 2015 by Daniella Blechner

All rights reserved. This book or any portion thereof
may not be reproduced or used in any manner whatsoever
without the express written permission of the publisher
except for the use of brief quotations in a book review.

Printed in the United Kingdom

First Printing 2015. Conscious Dreams Publishing. Daniella Blechner.

ISBN

www.daniellablechner.com
www.dingdongitsmrwrong.com

7 Steps to Creating the Greatest Version of YOU

Daniella Blechner

Introduction

7 Steps to Creating the Greatest Version of YOU will equip you with essential tools for living a more positive and empowered life. We all have an Inner Power and Inner Knowing and Inner Strength and sometimes, unfortunate circumstances, situations and negative belief systems cloud our judgement and block our energy channels which in turn prevents us from receiving the things that we deserve and desire.

We all deserve good things; we were all created to feel good. We were born to succeed in our dreams and to fulfil our desires no matter how small or large, however sometimes we are our own worst enemy and tell ourselves that, "we do not deserve it" or "somebody out there deserves it more." We all deserve to be fulfilled. We all have access to and the ability to attract that which we desire into our lives. We all deserve to live happy and healthy lives.

This Work Book is designed to help you assess your values and priorities. It will teach you to identify your needs, wants and desires as well as release and unblock old ways of thinking that may be acting as obstacles keeping you from getting what you want from life.

You will draw in maximum happiness when you are in alignment with the Greatest Version of You.

7 Steps to Creating the Greatest Version of YOU by Daniella Blechner

The 7 Steps Acronym to remember is:

What are my Values?
Own my Needs Wants and Desires
Manifest my Intentions
Exercise Forgiveness
Nightly Gratitude
Re-awaken my Vision
♥ Love Live Laugh

These are the 7 Steps to Creating the Greatest Version of YOU.

You are the author of your destiny and with these practical steps, you will not only put yourself on a positive path and change the course of your journey but will adjust your energy allowing space for all that you desire to enter your life. We all have the potential to do this. This is about mind-set, focus and continual practise on the right things.

We may desire a tropical holiday in the Caribbean but if we fritter away our money on bags and shoes, that holiday is not going to happen unless we suddenly get lucky playing the lottery! Our actions must be in alignment with our thoughts and intentions as well as our needs, wants and desires.

This workshop is about identifying who you are, what you value and need in order to live a fulfilling life. It's about challenging mind-sets and letting go of old world views. It is not about manifesting a tall, dark handsome millionaire, although that is certainly possible.

Attracting what's right for you requires inner work. It requires getting to know You by tuning in to the deepest inclination of your heart, the place of Power and the point from which you will make the transition from accepting what's thrown at you and requesting what you want, what you deserve, what's rightfully yours from the Universe.

Step 1: What Are My Values?

Everyone has values and these values vary from person to person. The word "value" derives from the Old French, feminine past participle of *valoir* 'be worth' and originates from the Latin *valere*. Values are the core beliefs and principles that you live by or a personal "moral code". Just as the word value comes from the word "worth" our values should reflect what we deem to be worthy.

How many of us have focussed on or have been influenced by society's ideals of having a "tall, dark and handsome" time and time again and ended up with a good looking Mr Wrong? Are we focussing on just the exterior, and perhaps more importantly, why are we focussing on just the exterior? Do we have deeper values beyond that, values which we may be ignoring? How clear are you on your own values? It's easy to assume that Mr Good-Looking will treat you like a Princess and be the man of your dreams, however how important is getting to know a man and examining his values and beliefs about love and relationships?

When you identify your values you will be better equipped to attract men who reflect these values. I once went on a few dates with a guy who I got on with very well. On date 3 he told me that he would disown his own son if he found out he was gay. Seeing that he was deadly serious, I knew I could not continue dating this man. To me, support, love and acceptance of our loved ones for who they are, without judgement, is very high up on my list of values. It is essential for me to be with someone who loves their children unconditionally. This told me that anything that goes against his own limited beliefs of what he thought was 'right' warranted punishment. Even though I thought he was a great person (bar this) and was physically attracted to him, I could never be with someone who was okay with abandoning their own child. Love should not be conditional and certainly should not be withheld from your own children. This completely went against my own value system and there was never a date 4!

Having very similar values is fundamental to compatibility. It's one of the key elements that hold us together. We may not have identical values to our partner's however respecting each other's values is essential. Remember, just as the word 'value' means worth, it's important to find someone who sees your values and beliefs as worthy of respect just as you are worthy, too.

Table of Values

Use the table below to help you decide upon your Top Ten values.

Acceptance	Accessibility	Accomplishment	Adaptability	Affection
Approachability	Assertiveness	Assurance	Attentiveness	Awareness
Belonging	Bliss	Bravery	Calmness	Care
Clarity	Closeness	Commitment	Community	Compassion
Completion	Composure	Confidence	Connection	Consciousness
Contentment	Contribution	Cooperation	Courage	Courtesy
Credibility	Curiosity	Dependability	Depth	Desire
Diligence	Discipline	Drive	Duty	Effectiveness
Empathy	Encouragement	Endurance	Energy	Enjoyment
Excellence	Excitement	Expressiveness	Exuberance	Fairness
Family	Fearlessness	Fierceness	Fitness	Flexibility
Focus	Fortitude	Freedom	Friendliness	Friendship
Generosity	Giving	Grace	Gratitude	Growth
Happiness	Harmony	Health	Helpfulness	Honesty
Hopefulness	Humour	Imagination	Independence	Individuality
Inspiration	Integrity	Intelligence	Intimacy	Introspection
Involvement	Joy	Kindness	Learning	Liveliness
Love	Loyalty	Maturity	Meaning	Mindfulness
Open-minded	Openness	Optimism	Organisation	Patience
perceptiveness	Perseverance	Persistence	Playfulness	Pleasure
Reasonableness	Reflection	Relaxation	Reliability	Resilience
Responsibility	Restraint	Reverence	Satisfaction	Security
Selflessness	Self-reliance	Sexuality	Simplicity	Sincerity
Spirituality	Stability	Strength	Success	Support
Thankfulness	Thoroughness	Thoughtfulness	Trust	Truth
Usefulness	Virtue	Willingness	Wisdom	Wonder

What are My Values?

As you write down the values, think about where you need and want to experience more of this value in your life.

1) _____

2) _____

3) _____

4) _____

5) _____

6) _____

7) _____

8) _____

9) _____

10) _____

Now look at these values you have written and ask yourself how you are exercising or demonstrating these values in your own life.

E.g. 1)

Value	How do I demo this value?	How can I demo this more?	How would having more of this value make you feel?
Respect	I show respect to my colleagues and friends by listening to their ideas, views and opinions.	I can respect my children more by listening to their feelings. I could also take the time to listen to my partner.	Validated, listened to and accepted.
Clarity	I demonstrate clarity in my instructions conveyed to colleagues and employees.	I do not always ask for what I want in a relationship. This causes confusion. I need more clarity.	Safe. Understood. Happy that communication is positive.

If we look at the table we can see that the values that we hold the highest are not always reflected in our actions. I believe if we want more Love in our loves, we need to demonstrate Love. Similarly, if we want more peace in our lives, we ourselves must demonstrate peace in all of our actions and interactions with others. Sometimes we may demonstrate these things but subconsciously block ourselves from receiving due to a deep seated belief that we do not deserve or that we are unworthy.

We don't have to necessarily start a long, arduous investigation into why we may feel that way or what happened to us along our journey, we can simply work on changing how we use our energy, how we direct it and how we harness it. This is where EFT comes in.

What is EFT?

EFT (Emotional Freedom Technique) is a practise that releases blockages in the flow of energy in the human organism.

Human energy is real. It's measurable and visible using the proper scientific instruments. The energy that is evident within DNA is luminescent. It emits actual light without the need of heat or an external power source. DNA carries genetic information that defines all your physical characteristics, but DNA is fluid, not fixed as was previously believed. Genes can be "coerced" into expressing different outcomes simply by changing the way we live, changing our lifestyle and the way we think about life.

EFT involves tapping on the major meridian points to shift and release energy that has stagnated due to the internalising of negative or limited beliefs. Thoughts, emotions and behaviours are all related to your energy and your ability to create outcomes through focussed manipulation. Tapping certain points will release whatever is causing the clog in the same way we might tap a tube of liquid to allow an air bubble to escape. In this way, with your energy freed up, you will be able to work on rebuilding yourself in the best way you can imagine.

Meridian Points

There are 13 meridian points to tap on. See diagram below.

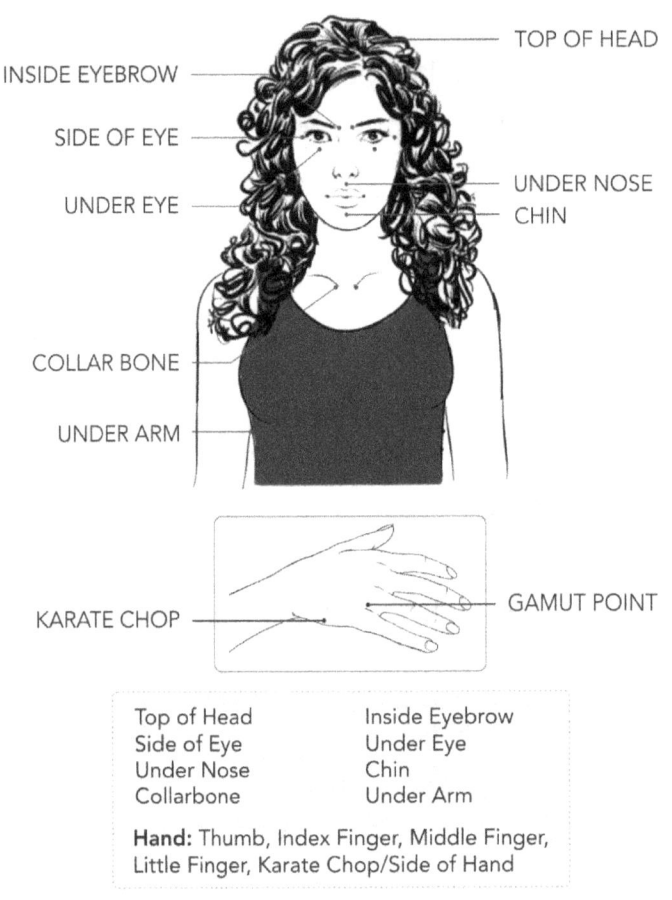

Using the values we have ranked the highest, we can use POSITIVE EFT. **Dr. Silvia Hartmann**, CEO of the Association for Meridian & Energy Therapies (the AMT) and a team of her senior trainers developed Energy EFT in 2011. Taking concepts, new techniques and brilliant insights from Energy EFT, Silvia created Positive EFT in 2013. Positive EFT focuses on empowering everyone right here and right now with tools that create a bright, compelling present and future regardless of one's past. [1]

---

[1] Taken from www.eft-md.com/home/positive

How to Get Going

Assume the Heart position. Stand with your feet slightly apart and place your hand on your heart. Take a few deep breaths and take note of how you are feeling in your mind, body and emotions. Name the value you are tapping on and see how it feels in your body. Note down how you feel on a scale of -10 to 10+
You are ready to start the round of tapping

By tapping on the meridian points using our set up statements, you will begin to increase and shift the flow of energy in your system.

If we want more love in our lives we can use set up statements such as:

I want more Love in my Life
Love is easy. It flows in abundance
It's safe to Love

As you go through the round of tapping or even halfway through, your statements may organically change according to how you are feeling. This is okay. Just keep focussing on the value you are tapping for. Whilst you are tapping, you may feel slight movements and shifts in your body, you may feel looser or start to yawn as a form of release. Don't question what happens or worry if you feel nothing at all. The work is being done.

After each round of tapping assume the Heart position, take a few deep breaths and check in. On a scale of -10 to 10+ note how you feel.

You can use Positive EFT for any aspect of your Life and the beauty of it is you can create and change the statements to whatever you want. The Power is with You! Try and find a time to in-cooperate this practise in your daily routine and you'll see some fabulous changes that may include better sleep, less anxiety or restlessness, more clarity of mind, more physical energy that's light but not erratic, better memory, and a balanced appetite!

Step 2: Owning Our Needs, Wants and Desires

Needs, wants and desires are very essential in relationships. Everybody has needs, wants and desires that they would like to be fulfilled. The question is how often do we remember them? Have they ever been written down? In some cases they haven't even been recognised or identified until we are treated badly.

What are the Differences between Needs, Wants and Desires?

Needs are essential prerequisites that are required to survive in a situation. They are the basics as it were, something we literally cannot do without. For example, we need air to breath and food to sustain us, and in the context of a relationship, we all have a basic need to be loved and a basic need for respect.

Wants are things we would like to have but can survive without. For example, I want a car but as I live in London and am close to an abundance of transport links I do not NEED one desperately. Wants in relationships are not essential to physical survival but are essential to emotional and spiritual well-being. We can want certain qualities in a relationship, so we will learn now how choosing and setting intentions regarding the kind of relationship and partner we want is well within our power.

Desires are add-ons, things we really, really want but that are not necessary for our survival or our happiness. They are luxuries, the icing on the cake that we crave and deep down dream of and yearn for. For example I desire to go to Cuba this summer, visit Brazil and camp out in the Amazon, however practicalities and real life means that I may not necessarily get to do these things. Desires are something to aim for and never give up on.

Look at the example exercise on the next page and try it for yourself. Don't worry if you become stuck or are not sure what you need, want and desire.

This exercise will get you thinking and setting your expectations and intentions. Go for it! You deserve to be fulfilled!

Exercise
Needs, Wants and Desires

What Do I Need?

I need a partner who respects me.
I need a partner who is reliable.
I need a partner who is kind and generous, loving and affectionate.

I need a relationship that is equal.
I need a relationship that is based on trust.
I need a relationship that is happy and healthy.

What Do I Want?

I want a partner who will take me out on dates regularly.
I want a partner listens to me compassionately.
I want a partner who supports and encourages me.

I want a relationship that has plenty of laughter.
I want a relationship that is full of passion.
I want a relationship where each other listens

What Do I Desire?

I desire a partner who pampers me with massages and foot rubs once in a while.
I desire a partner who takes me out on romantic dates.
I desire a partner who enjoys travelling to exotic locations with me.

I desire a relationship that is full of romance, passion and love.
I desire a peaceful yet exciting romantic relationship that results in a long term marriage.
I desire a relationship where we travel extensively and enjoy exploring all corners of the Earth.

Exercise
Needs, Wants and Desires

What Do I Need?

I need a partner who _____.
I need a partner who _____.
I need a partner who _____.

I need a relationship _____.
I need a relationship _____.
I need a relationship _____.

What Do I Want?

I want a partner who _____.
I want a partner who _____.
I want a partner who _____.

I want a relationship _____.
I want a relationship _____.
I want a relationship _____.

What Do I Desire?

I desire a partner who _____.
I desire a partner who _____.
I desire a partner who _____.

I desire a relationship _____.
I desire a relationship _____.
I desire a relationship _____.

What's Next?

It's a good idea to keep checking in with your Needs, Wants and Desires and take note of where they are or are not being met. Remember that whilst it's great to keep this exercise in a safe place don't keep them in a safe; Ask for What You Need. Equally, like the Values Exercise, take note as to where and how you are exercising these Needs, Wants and Desires with others too.

The world acts as a mirror and within it must be balance and equilibrium.

Step 3: Manifest My Intentions

Now that you have established your Needs, Wants and Desires, let's begin setting your intentions. Each of us has so many good intentions, hopes and dreams for our lives yet sometimes it seems nearly impossible to attain them. We spend so much time focussing on our problems and obstacles that we forget to leave room for that which we desire and intend for our lives. We lose sight of our values and our hope wanes as we become distracted with day to day problems.

Intentions are crucial if we choose to walk in our purpose and live the Life we want.

You have joined this workshop because there are things you want to achieve and have more of to live an empowered Life. You have an idea about the kind of life you want but you haven't crystalised a vision for it. You don't know how to make vision into reality.

The Needs, Wants and Desires exercise has helped you identify your Needs, Wants and Desires and now these must be affirmed in daily practise. Voicing your intentions speaks a message to the Universe that's loud and clear about the things that are of value and importance to you.

Extract from Mr Wrong Chapter 9-Start With You

Setting Your Intentions

"An intention is a higher- consciousness thought. It is a desire expressed with absolute faith that the outcome will transpire. An intention is an expectation simply handed over to the Universe in order for it to be fulfilled—a bit like placing an order at a restaurant and then waiting for the meal to arrive. When we place the order or express the intention, we expect the meal to arrive. We don't hound and harass or follow the waiter into the kitchen to ensure they have placed the order correctly or get into the kitchen and start cooking it ourselves. We have faith that the order will arrive. Just as we say thank you when we place our order and again when our order arrives, we must do the same with our intentions. Gratitude plays a major role in intention setting."

I strongly suggest you write down your intentions. This helps keep you focussed especially when you may start to feel you are losing hope. Keep your intentions in a peaceful place; one that is sacred to you. I have mine stuck on a wall dedicated to progression in my room. It's a good idea to have intentions that relate to each part of your Life be it: Career, Family, Love and Relationships, Health, Wealth, Property or Personal Development.

Here are some of my Intentions:

I attract an abundance of Love, Peace, Harmony, Wealth, Joy and Happiness.
I am full of Energy, Vibrancy and Good Health.
I am Open to receiving Love.
The World is a beautiful place and I am exploring it all with excitement.

7 Steps to Creating the Greatest Version of YOU by Daniella Blechner

Post It Note Exercise

No one fully understands the powerful potential of the human brain, but the fact is that your brain doesn't know the difference between a real experience and a virtual one. That's why all the bad relationships you've had are so deeply impressed in your mind and continue to work against you in each and every relationship. The experience is not really happening, but your mind expects it to happen because that is the reality you've created for it. When it does happen, the expectation is reinforced.

In the same way, you can literally think your way to any new experience you intend. Your brain will see this as a real experience and expect the same thing in the next relationship.

So, let's get manifesting!

Using the Post-Its on the next page, write down your intentions. Make sure you use the, "I am" or "I have" form. Using the present tense causes the subconscious to believe it the intent has already manifested, that it actually happened and was a real experience. These thought patterns attract energy that resonates on the same vibration as like attracts like.

Your intentions can be as simple as wanting to have better posture or they can be something that will result in a pivotal moment for you. They can be anything but you must be clear and specific about what your intention is. It's not enough to simply say "I want a better life".

Read your intentions aloud. You can read them once, twice three times or even sing them. How you choose to read them is up to you. As you read them, try to imagine how it feels to have this manifested.

- Visualise it actually happening.
- If you are sensitive to energy, note down how reading each intention affects your energy.
- What sensations are you experiencing?
- Do you feel them in your physical energy or as emotional energy?

Don't try and work anything out, just make a mental note and continue reading. Sometimes I have to read an intention three or four times to let it really sink in. Declare it to the world and when you have finished, always say Thank You.

Do this with passion and dedication to getting where you want to be in your life. Make the commitment to work for this. Your life is worth it. The only way to create the future you want for yourself is by distilling everything you want into those words that make up your intention - what you want to see happen for you - and by believing and accepting that it's all there for you.

At 17 I read Iyanla Vanzant's book *One Day My Soul Just Opened Up*. In it she says that she always ends her declarations and intentions with "For This I Am So Grateful! And So It Is!" This struck a real chord with me and I have been using it ever since. What these words do is send out a message that you have absolute faith that the Universe will deliver. Having gratitude for all that we receive even before it is delivered is a crucial part of the process. Verbalising words of gratitude as you feel this gratitude makes it doubly powerful.

Here's what happens when you say Thank You. You acknowledge the Universe as your co-worker. You are grateful for that help, for the ability to clearly see what you want, and for the successful outcome - the actual manifestation - of what you intended, reinforcing this as a real experience in your subconscious and reminding you that everything out there with your name on it is waiting for you to ask for it.

My Intentions

Step 4: Exercise Forgiveness

One of the keys to living a freer, happier and lighter life is lies in your ability and willingness to forgive. Forgiveness is such an easy word to say but sometimes so hard to do. Read the excerpt below from Mr Wrong.

Love Bless and Release

"Sometimes we experience so much pain we find it difficult to let go. We find it difficult to forgive and move on leaving us stuck in a negative cycle. Whatever the reason is, we are weighed down and filled with bitterness, resentment, anger, disappointment and regret whilst whoever hurt us is walking around as light as a feather or perhaps continuing to treat others in the same hurtful way. Why are we carrying around their baggage? Hurt and pain are only inflicted as a result of others' insecurities. Ladies why are we carrying these bags??! What's in the past is in the past and must stay there! This is easier said than done. Sometimes we carry this burden - and believe you me I've carried a heavy load for a long, long time (probably the cause of my back pain) - because we are afraid to let go.

We may feel that if we let go we are allowing the other person to "get away with it" or that we have become a "walkover" somehow by forgetting about it. But in essence what we are doing is quite the opposite; we are finally moving on without the load, without the negative thoughts and feelings eroding our backs, our emotions and our Souls. We also may feel that we cannot let go as we remain nostalgic about the past. The abuse or pain we endured becomes less "valid" if we let it go. We've allowed it to define us in some way and we don't want to forget it. But in actual fact what it's doing is making us move slower, making us weaker, bitter and lonely. Let that traumatic and painful part of your journey not define you but serve as a tool to help you grow stronger and wiser, happier and lighter. Again, easier said than done.

Remember, forgiving does not mean forgetting. It does not mean letting them back into your lives with the same circumstances or at all for that matter. It means seeing that person as a human being who's made some terrible mistakes but helped you grow in some way whether it was emotionally, physically, mentally or spiritually. For in every challenge or difficulty there is strength and wisdom to be gained. It means releasing that person and their negative energy. It also means releasing the negative energy you've internalised and freeing yourself. It means forgiving yourself for not feeling strong enough, being wise enough to react or act differently at the time. Once forgiveness is achieved you can finally take the next step to finding true happiness and Mr Right. Without forgiveness you will keep attracting the same circumstances, same lessons and same type of person into our lives until forgiveness is learnt."

Now are you ready to forgive?

Think of someone who has hurt you. When you think of them, how do you feel in your body? Do your muscles start to tense up, does your throat become blocked with repressed emotion or does your brain start ticking about all the injustices you endured? Now is the time to let it go.

What do you need to forgive them for?

E.g. 1) I forgive you for not being there when I needed you.

Your Forgiveness List

1) _____

2) _____

3) _____

4) _____

5) _____

6) _____

7) _____

Now think about how holding this has made you feel over the weeks, months or years. The body, mind and spirit are not separate. Every negative emotion that takes place in the mind is felt in the body and in the spirit. It pollutes every experience and can start to wreak havoc in your cells. It also blocks the flow of energy, creating stagnation, like sludge, in your system. By sending healing messages of forgiveness, you will focus on correct instructions for the future, in essence untangling all the hurts and fears and wrong messages that your brain has experienced.

If we could see the damage unforgiveness causes we would be apologising and forgiving ourselves. When we start to forgive ourselves we start to take ownership for what happened to us and recognise how we can act as our own angels. We can guide our own stories onto positive paths without repeating our victim story. What we are angry about is not so much the actual action itself but how it made us feel.

"You become what you think about most, but you also attract what you think about most." - John Assaraf

I Forgive Myself For...

1) Allowing your behaviour to affect me in a negative way, for letting that negativity dictate how I feel about myself and for the stories I have created about my reality as a result. I believed I needed you and forgot the power I was born with to be there for myself.

2) _____

3) _____

4) _____

5) _____

6) _____

7) _____

One of my favourite quotes is from visionary guide and spiritual teacher Sonia Choquette.

"Forgive and forget all that has hurt you in the past and made you doubt your own "lovability". Realise that hurt and disappointment are inevitable parts of our human learning experience. No matter how painful, the real injury was not that someone didn't cherish you, but that you erroneously believed you didn't deserve to be loved."

- Soul Lessons and Soul Purpose Oracle Cards- Sonia Choquette

Other Forgiveness Exercises

1) Write a letter to the person who has hurt you letting you know how you feel. When you have finished. Imagine them receiving it and fully listening and understanding what you have written with compassion and asking for your forgiveness. Let it go. Burn or throw away the letter. You are done. Keeping the letter keeps the negative emotions and energy alive.

2) Imagine a scenario where you are face to face with this person. Create a warm and peaceful atmosphere. Before you speak look into their eyes and seek understanding and compassion. See their life, their hardships their struggles, see their beauty as well as their ugly behaviour, and see their pain as well as their triumphs. They are human just like you. Now tell them softly why you are hurting and how their actions or behaviour made you feel. See them listening to every word you say, taking it in. You have been heard and understood. You see in their eyes that somewhere along the lines, they too have been hurt and were only acting on and operating from their own level of understanding and painful experiences. Softly, they ask for your forgiveness and this is all you require. You accept. It is done. Peacefully, you both rise up, smile and walk your separate ways.

3) **Ho'oponopono** (ho-o-pono-pono) is an ancient Hawaiian practice of reconciliation and forgiveness. It is defined in the Hawaiian dictionary as "mental cleansing." Ponopono is defined as "to put to rights; to put in order or shape, correct, revise, adjust, amend, regulate, arrange, rectify, tidy up, make orderly or neat" [1]

---

[1] Cited from Wikipedia

How to do it: **Ho'oponopono** is a very simple ancient mantra which can be done by repeating this simple cycle of statements:

I Love You,
I'm Sorry,
Please Forgive Me,
Thank You

The purpose behind this is to reflect the belief that our purpose here is to let go and allow Love to solve our problems. Sound Good? Give it a whirl!

Step 5: Nightly Gratitude

Gratitude is paramount. It sends a clear message out to the world that we are grateful for all that we have received. As a strong believer in God, every night I send prayers of thank you for every positive in my Life. I thank God for all my life experiences no matter how traumatic or painful as I can see that, through them, I have learned and evolved; my Soul has become richer. I ask God to give me the courage and the Strength to use my adversities and transform them into ways to help inspire and empower others.

I know that not everyone has a belief in God and that is fine. Gratitude can be sent into the Universe, absorbed by the Universal energy we exist in and reflected back to us. The positive energy connected to Gratitude sends out a message that we acknowledge and appreciate what we have been given and are ready to receive more positive things into our lives. It is equally important to show that we have learned from our mistakes, struggles and experiences. Why? It brings a sense of Peace and completion.

There is an ebb and flow to Life and when we fail to acknowledge the learning we fail to grow. Instead we sink into the role of the victim. When you play the role of "victim" then that is the message you send out to the Universe and everything in it about who you are, who you've declared yourself to be. When you expect people to hurt you and treat you badly, you send out the same vibrations of victimhood. When you operate from victimhood, self-fulfilling prophecies about "life never going right" and "being screwed over again" become realities. This becomes your world view and the point from which you operate, not only in love relationships, but in business, friendships, family and your relationship with yourself. Remember, the brain doesn't know the difference between a real experience and a virtual one.

Every bad experience presents me with an opportunity to change my mind set. For this I am So Grateful!!

Excerpt from Mr Wrong Chapter 11- The Power of Forgiveness

Gratitude

"No matter how badly someone has treated us in the past, we can always find some positives. If we are still struggling to forgive, it is a good idea to start focussing not on what they have done wrong but on the things they have done right. Make a list of things they have done right or things they have done that have made you feel good. This not only raises your energy by focussing on the positive but also brings into your consciousness feel-good thoughts and feelings associated with that person to counteract the negative, making them a far less toxic person in your mind. Before or after each positive sentence, write "I thank you." Look at the examples below.

I thank you for being a fantastic father to my children.
I thank you for supporting and encouraging me in my career.
I thank you for all the happy memories you helped me create.
I thank you for making me laugh when I was down.
I thank you for helping me through my relative's death.
I thank you for letting me wear your jacket even though you were freezing yourself.

There is so much power in gratitude and being grateful. We have so much to be grateful for—even through the seemingly dark times. Again, just because you write a list of positive things about a person who has hurt you it doesn't mean you should suddenly forget what has happened and go back to them. It does mean you have changed your perspective of an experience and therefore you've changed your present condition. You've turned something negative into something positive.

This will help you look objectively at this person as a whole, as a multifaceted being with many layers human layers. It will help you connect with all that is good and do away with the toxic elements of the connection. You must be grateful for the experience you have had, let it go and make room for more positive experiences in your life."

Who Needs more Gratitude in your Life?

Think about someone you may be out of sync with. They may have hurt you, you may feel angry towards them or perhaps you need to forgive them. Try listing the positive things they have contributed to your Life. This exercise will help you gain some perspective and focus on the positive aspects they are bringing into your Life. When you focus on the positive aspects you will attract more of that positive energy. Give it a Go!

I Thank You

_____
_____
_____
_____
_____
_____
_____
_____
_____
_____
_____

Now make a List of all the things you are Grateful For:

_____

1. _____

_____

2. _____

_____

3. _____

_____

4. _____

_____

5. _____

_____

6. _____

_____

7. _____

_____

8. _____
_____

9. _____
_____

10. _____
_____

11. _____
_____

12. _____
_____

13. _____
_____

14. _____
_____

15. _____
_____

16. _____
_____

17. _____
_____

18. _____
_____

19. _____
_____

20. _____
_____

21. _____
_____

22. _____
_____

23. _____
_____

24. _____
_____

25. _____
_____

26. _____
_____

27. _____
_____

28. _____
_____

29. _____
_____

30. _____
_____

31. _____
_____

32. _____
_____

33. _____
_____

34. _____
_____

35. _____
_____

36. _____
_____

37. _____
_____

38. _____
_____

39. _____
_____

40. _____
_____

41. _____
_____

42. _____
_____

43. _____
_____

44. _____
_____

45. _____
_____

46. _____
_____

47. _____
_____

48. _____
_____

49. _____
_____

50. _____
_____

Look at your list. How does it make you feel? Do your setbacks and desires pale in comparison? Read your list nightly to remind yourself just how blessed you truly are.

As long as I can remember I prayed to God and spoke out loud to the Universe. Whenever I am in the depths of despair, I always start with this.

> Dear God (substitute Universe, Creator, Source of All Things or whatever you believe to be the blessing behind your existence)
>
> I am alive. I am so grateful for my good health. I have two eyes that work, a nose, a mouth; I have a voice, a body that moves when I want it to, two feet that can walk, two hands that can feel, a heart, a head and an array of emotions. My body houses my Soul and my Soul is deathless, timeless. This is just an experience and I show you my upmost gratitude for it. It may be hard, it may be tough but I'm alive. I thank you for giving me the Strength of my ancestors who faced struggles and hardships that, thankfully, I can't even begin to imagine. I am so wondrously in awe of all that they endured, battled and overcame so that I may stand here today; with a voice, a strong mind and power to exercise my rights. I will never be short of water, food, drink or shelter. Whatever I may be suffering thank you that it is only temporary. I am looking forward to better days and so much more.
>
> I am a strong believer that whatever tragedy we may be facing or set back we may be experiencing, there's always space for gratitude and new things to grow.

What would your Prayer of Gratitude be when battling a storm?

Dear _____

_____
_____
_____
_____
_____
_____
_____
_____
_____
_____
_____
_____

Re read your list aloud and read out your Prayer or meditation. Do you feel your energy change as you voice your Gratitude? Now that is Power![1]

---

1   *NB Sometimes we can get so swept away with expressing our Gratitude that we have no desire to ask for anything. This is no bad thing!

7 Steps to Creating the Greatest Version of YOU by Daniella Blechner

Step 6: Reawaken my Vision

Visualisation is another key to manifesting that which we desire. I am a very visual person. I dream in vivid visuals, I think in visuals and as a child sitting in the classroom I was able to visualise the speaker's aura, tell you exactly what they were wearing and talk in detail about the colours and energy the speaker exuded. Unfortunately, I found it hard to focus in lectures and could not listen to people speaking for a long period of time- I couldn't tell you a word they said but could mimic the exact intonation and tone of voice they used. There would be a visual synergy to it.

Before every event, every achievement and every important occasion, I visualise it. I imagine what it would be like to experience my Dreams coming true. Once I live it in my mind, the reality becomes stronger; it's already happened.

You have now established your values, recognised your Needs, Wants and Desires and set your Intentions. The final stage is Visualisation. Read the extract from Mr Wrong below on Vision Boards. This is what we are going to create!

Vision Boards

> *"Vision boards are a collection of images placed on a board. The images can be drawn or selected from magazines, papers or adverts but must represent all things positive you wish to manifest into your life. For example if you are looking for marriage, stick images of beautiful brides and grooms, wedding rings and dresses on your board. If you want more money stick images of pots of gold or notes. If you wish to own property abroad, flick through travel brochures or property brochures and select images of houses you wish to own in the future. Stick all these on your vision board and place it somewhere you will regularly look at it, perhaps just before bed and before waking up. Use your affirmations and intentions and focus upon them while studying the images. For example if*

you want to attract a man who owns a yacht, loves children and can offer a woman all the love, security, respect and honesty she deserves...oh, as well as a ring... then focus upon him and focus upon your intentions.

It can also work for making changes from within. If you want to gain more money or heal from a past situation set your intention; "I have an abundance of money," or "I am healed and happy." Gratitude is extremely important and so as we finish setting our intentions we must have absolute faith that it will arrive and give thanks to the Universe or your subconscious brain for making it happen. Now whether you believe in miracles or not is another book, however one thing can be said with the utmost confidence and that is these positive affirmations train your brain to think differently about yourself and life itself. They train your brain to start thinking positively about love and relationships, to release negative belief systems and to focus upon that which gives you joy and complete happiness. Try it today!"

Representation

When you are creating your vision board make sure you are using images that represent you. When I first started to create my vision board, I realised that the absence of images of people who represented me - a mixed race female of Caribbean and European heritage - was having a great effect on my ability to visualise as well as on my personal feelings about my self-image and worth. As I searched through the various Wedding and Brides magazine, I found myself switching off as there was not one single 'person of colour' I could relate to within it. I realised that the absence of these positive images subconsciously programmed a belief system within me that marriage was not for me.

When we see images of those who represent our visual or racial makeup we are instantly attracted to the image as it forms a connection or association within us. The same goes for gender and even body type. I am a real lover of Positive Black Images and Black Art as the emphasis is heavily upon a Strong family unit where mothers are seen as Goddesses and Queens and men as Protective Kings. Maybe it was the ABSENCE of these images that had been subconsciously conditioning my thinking. I have always ensured that I fill my house with positive images where women, family and Black culture are celebrated.

Begin to create and visualise yourself using positive images that reflect your values, your appearance or the appearance to which you aspire, and the surroundings and circumstances you want to find yourself.

If there is an absence of images that represent you, create them. If you are a 20 year old young woman of Black heritage and want to visualise success, don't stick up a picture of 40+ suited and booted Caucasian men sat in a boardroom. Think about YOU. Where are you in that picture? What do you represent? What does success mean to you? What colours do you see? What energy do YOU bring? Start creating. You will be taking in these images every day and so it is imperative that these images closely match Who YOU are. If you cannot find yourself in mainstream media visuals, paint yourself in, mentally and physically. Train your brain to break down invisible barriers and don't hold back. YOU can dream or you can DREAM. Paint any picture. Create the visual and start visualising. Start believing for what you want.

Now let's summarise Steps 1-6 so far

Top Ten Tips
- Look back at your values; ensure you are upholding these values yourself
- Align yourself with people and situations that reflect these values
- Read your Needs, Wants and Desires every morning
- Remember to Ask for what you Need, Want and Desire. No one is a mind reader!
- Vocalise your Intentions daily
- Imagine the feeling of receiving what you have asked for
- Demonstrate Nightly Gratitude
- Forgive those who have hurt you
- Forgive yourself for mistakenly believing you are unworthy
- Visualise your Intentions

Step 7: ♥ Love. Live. Laugh.

What I've come to realise is that Life really is short. It can be taken away from us without a moment's notice and suddenly, not getting that job, being cheated on or that argument with the ex becomes null and void. We think that we will live forever and that we are invincible; that our lives and what happens in them is so important. When this is all taken away or threatened, we realise that very few things are important. When I die I want God to ask me, "Did you Live enough?" "Did you Love enough? Did you allow enough LOVE in? Did you learn to forgive? Did you Laugh enough? Did you have Fun?" For these are the basis of every bit of positivity we can create within our lives. Passing a bit of Love onto another, even a stranger, can make their day. It can determine whether they take their lives that evening or tell someone they love them; it can determine whether they scream at their employees or bring cookies in to raise morale. We underestimate the power of a smile.

At one point or other we have all been saints or sinners. That's not the beauty of contrast. It's how we react to stress that brings out the best or worst in us. It's normal to feel down at times and it's normal to sometimes be irrational but when we have a chance to be happy, embrace it with both hands. My motto for work is "Unite. Inspire. Empower" but my motto for Life is "Live. Love. Laugh". Never underestimate the power of laughter. It raises our serotonin levels and creates buzzy feel good feelings, and the best thing about it is laughter is infectious.

I was always a big giggler and was always playing practical jokes and laughing at school. It's what keeps us young at heart. It raises our energy flow and level of happiness. And who doesn't want to be happy? Look for the humour in your adversities. It's the only way I've got through mine! Soul searching can be tough but it doesn't have to be arduous as long as we remember to Love, Live and Laugh. Happiness is truly the key to attracting positivity into our lives. Who's up for that?

7 Steps to Creating the Greatest Version of YOU by Daniella Blechner

Write down five things that make you happy.

1) _____

2) _____

3) _____

4) _____

5) _____

Did you...?

E.g. 1) Accept a compliment? *Yes, the postman told me he liked my new hair colour and it felt fricking awesome! Somebody noticed!*

1) Smile at a stranger today?
2) Do something you've never done before?
3) Make somebody laugh?
4) Appreciate nature?
5) Tell someone you loved them?
6) Accept a compliment?
7) Put yourself first?
8) Treat yourself to a self-care luxury?

9) _____

10) _____

11) _____

7 Steps to Creating the Greatest Version of YOU by Daniella Blechner

Write a List of 45 things to do before _____

_____

1. _____

2. _____

3. _____

4. _____

5. _____

6. _____

7. _____

8. _____

9. _____

10. _____

11. _____

12. _____

13. _____

14. _____

15. _____

16. _____

17. _____

18. _____

19. _____

20. _____

21. _____

22. _____

23. _____

24. _____

7 Steps to Creating the Greatest Version of YOU by Daniella Blechner

25. _____

26. _____

27. _____

28. _____

29. _____

30. _____

31. _____

32. _____

33. _____

34. _____

35. _____

36. _____

37. _____

38. _____

39. _____

40. _____

41. _____

42. _____

43. _____

44. _____

45. _____

7 Steps to Creating the Greatest Version of YOU by Daniella Blechner

Love. Live. Laugh

The more we turn our attention to positive things that make us feel good, the more open we are to receiving more positive vibrations, circumstances and people into our lives.

- Live your life.
- Learn from nature.
- Care for yourself deeply.
- Give Love freely
- Be open to receiving Love
- Demonstrate Kindness
- Have fun.

The more you Love and accept yourself the more you will exude a sense of self-worth. There is nothing more attractive than a woman, or man, who knows their true value. This is not arrogance but a quiet understanding that we have the freedom of choice to reflect all that is beautiful and positive within this world or not.

You are unique and there will never again be a person in this world quite like you, flaws, quirks and all.

We have a choice to value and honour this truth and celebrate our temporary place in this world or sink into negative thought patterns that create stories about who we are according to our past experiences, the experiences which we allowed to happen, whether they were the result of social bias, upbringing, ignorance or doubt. When we cut the negative ties to the past and learn from our experiences we become lighter and freer people with the ability to inspire and shine our light on others, and we give others the freedom to shine their own light. When we feel good about ourselves, listen to ourselves and take care of ourselves, we will begin to attract all that is positive into our lives. It's really that simple. It's a journey and we will never get it "right" all of the time, we may never feel "positive" and "happy" all of the time.

Don't allow yourself to stagnate when you don't get it right. Sit at the centre of your consciousness and see the situation for what it is. Think about where you could have made a different decision with a different outcome. Know that you created what happened and view it in the abstract, as something separate from yourself, not as a part of you that defines your worth. Let it go. Visualize how things might have turned out differently if you'd chosen a different reaction and then create better outcome so your brain will remember it for the next time. Smile, recognizing the power you possess.

By knowing who we are - what makes us happy, what we stand for - and knowing our True Value, we will never be in "pursuit of happiness" but consistently on the path to Joy.

You Draw in Maximum Happiness when you are in alignment with The Greatest Version of YOU!

Notes:

7 Steps to Creating the Greatest Version of YOU by Daniella Blechner

Notes:

www.ingramcontent.com/pod-product-compliance
Lightning Source LLC
Chambersburg PA
CBHW050718090526
44588CB00014B/2336